AN INSOMNIAC's

GUIDE TO THE SMALL HOURS

An INSOMNIAC's
GUIDE TO THE
SMALL HOURS

YSENDA MAXTONE GRAHAM · KATH WALKER

First published in 2012 by
Short Books, 3A Exmouth House, Pine Street
London EC1R 0JH

A CIP catalogue record for this book
is available from the British Library.
ISBN 978-1-78072-113-2

Printed in China by Hung Hing

1.03 am. The Wrong Position: 1.

Lying on the stomach, face turned sharp-right for breathing purposes, like someone coming up for air while swimming the crawl. Whole body pressing down into the mattress. Bosoms squished. Cheek jammed into the pillow. One nostril out of action. Mouth half-open. You've never, ever slept in this position, so what makes you think it's going to work this time?

You turn the pillow over and have a momentary Arctic sensation. Cold, fresh, delicious, like a snowy field. But all too soon, warm and sweaty.

Where can your arms go when you're lying like this? Not straight down, like a horizontal standing-to-attention. That would never work: too hot for wrists to be trapped under the duvet. Folded and tucked under the face is worth trying: arms making triangles like chicken wings.

It's boiling, even though the window's wide open. Did you choose the wrong tog-factor? The sales assistant in the duvet department did say it was an autumn-to-winter one. No one buys two duvets, surely? Where would you store the other one for six months of the year?

Do you turn your head towards your husband or away from him?

Away. How sad is that? In a double bed, married, still in love, but turned away. As far away as possible, in fact, if either of you hope to get any sleep. You need the space. The British aerospace. The other person's breathing, or, worse still, breath, is anathema to sleep.

You've even swapped the king-size bed for a super-king, with separate mattresses which aren't zipped together. More space, and a rift. Anything, anything to stop you being awake at 1.15am as you are now. So it hasn't worked. £800 badly spent, and you now have the burden of having to 'turn' the new mattress every three weeks, as hard to remember as worming the dog. (Jan, April, July, Oct. Did you remember? Is that why she's been scraping her bottom along the floor recently?)

Now he's snoring. The end of a cold. You did promise 'In sickness and in health'. He can't help it. No one can. You probably do it yourself. Prod him with the nearest leg. It stops for a minute as he surfaces, then starts again as he goes deeply back into his enviable man-sleep.

In films the lovers sleep cupped together. You never see James Bond and his girl waking up facing away from each other at opposite edges of the bed. Are you abnormal, or is James Bond?

Should you turn the radio on?

Arguments against: it might wake him up. Then there would be two insomniacs and it would be your fault. It might wake you up even more.

Arguments in favour: the background chat might send you back to sleep. It's company. The loneliness! Just to know there are other people in the world, even if they are at war. It's always war on the radio in the middle of the night. Misery, famine, rape, death in a far country.

You turn the volume down to zero, switch on to the World Service (the night bus of Radio 4), and turn up the volume until you can just hear it. Surely that won't wake him. Yes: a widowed mother in Somalia telling her appalling story.

He stirs. You turn the radio off. But now you can't stop thinking about war. It's time for the nightly dip into the Holocaust, which infests your thoughts. This was the time of night when the SS came to take families away. They knew everyone would be at home, the children tucked up in bed, deep in their dreams. Half an hour to pack a suitcase. How can anyone sleep in a world where that kind of thing has happened?

A good moment to plough on with the book-group book?

It's never the right moment to do that. You're bogged down in Chapter 4, where the author writes at length about her childhood on a ranch in the Canadian Rockies. Hell is other people's choice of book. Book-group night is approaching fast. Better switch the 40-watt insomniac bedside light on and get the page number up.

Will the lamp-light wake him? He stirs, turns briefly towards you (No! No! That's the wrong thing to do!), then turns away again and sinks back down with a somnolent sigh.

Lie on your side in the sleeping position, using his pillow to prop the book up. A thick, stocky paperback, the kind you almost have to break in half to open properly. Fine when you're on the bottom half of the right-hand page. But when you turn over to the top half of the left-hand page, it's much harder. Your hand isn't in a strong enough position to stop the book from falling forward and closing. Your eyes strain upwards, the words almost out of reach. All this effort so you can read about the wildlife Kathy saw on a memorable day's hiking with her sister in the 1970s. Is it worth it?

It's time to go to the loo.

That might help. No one can sleep with a full bladder. That might be what's stopping you. You get up – arms aching after being forced into that challenging book-holding position – and stumble to the bathroom. The blinding light! Halogen down-lights, hard to change the bulbs, a special twisting-and-pushing action. Wooden seat, one hinge broken, must go to B&Q, but at least it's warm – not like the black Bakelite one your grandmother had: that was freezing, and so was her tiled floor. The cold in those days!

Reading matter around the loo: a *Wisden Cricketers' Almanack*, open at 'Pakistan in England, 1974'; last week's *The Week*; *The Ladybird Book of Dogs*; Betjeman's poems. A family bathroom. To be someone's urinating and defecating reading-matter: how would an author like that?

A long pee: blame the camomile tea. It would be sobering to count up the number of times you need to 'go' in 24 hours. As many times as all the males in your family put together? That's the price you pay for having given birth to three of them. It's embarrassing when you're on holiday: forever going into cafés and museums and looking for international 'toilet' signs.

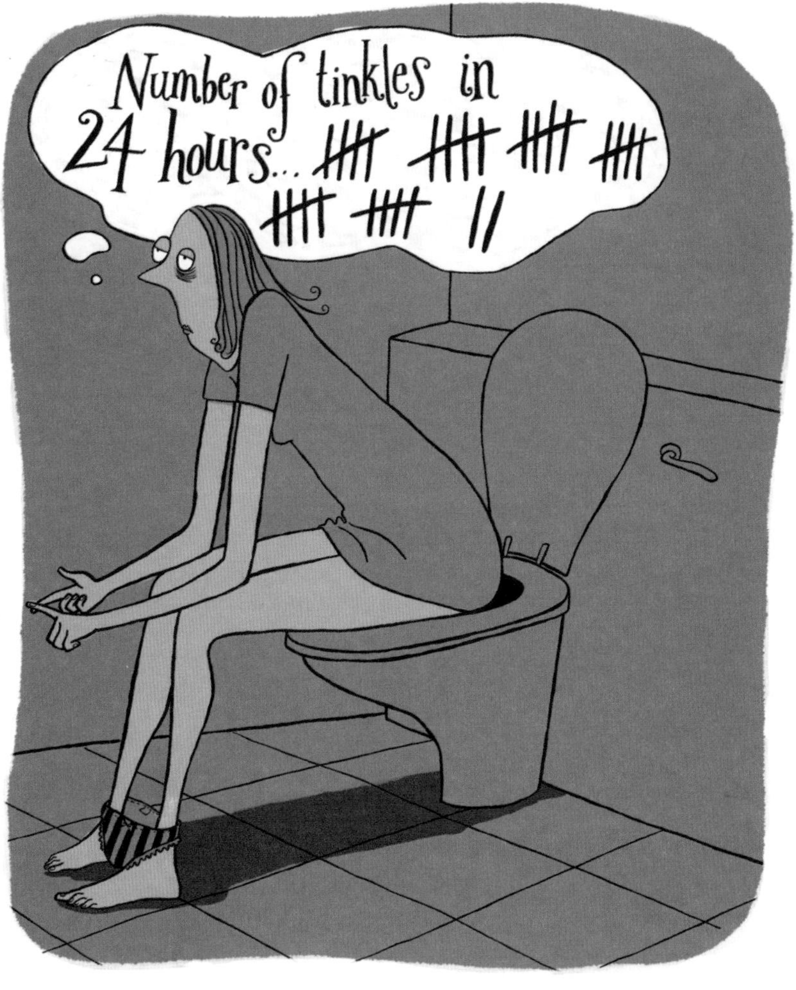
Number of tinkles in 24 hours... 𝍸 𝍸 𝍸 𝍸 𝍸 𝍸 ||

1:32 am. The Wrong Position: 2.

Lying on your back, like a knight on his tomb. Hands by your side this time, but on rather than under the duvet. Perhaps you should put them in the praying position like the knight. *Please God, grant me sleep.* You look dead. At least you feel thin, as this position exposes the ribs and hip bones. If only you hadn't had that pasta last night, heaped with tomato sauce and Parmesan, followed by two After Eights. Washed down with the dregs of the Chilean white. Pasta, cheese, chocolate and wine: all conducive to migraine and probably not good for sleep, either. But you can't sleep if you're too hungry. There must be a middle way.

Would you rather be a stone effigy at Canterbury Cathedral or a plaster-cast one in the Cast Court at the Victoria and Albert Museum?

The dripping tap.

But you did turn it off. As tight as it would go. The washer's gone. That black Polo-mint-shaped thing the plumber always shows you, flat and finished. The drip is annoying, but is it annoying enough to justify the plumber's call-out charge? You might need to wait for two other things to go wrong first. The loo seat doesn't count. Not a plumber's job.

The noise brings on the need to pee again. You stumble back to the bathroom and stuff a large flannel up the tap. That'll shut it up for a while. £75 an hour plus VAT, minimum time one hour. Pull a Kleenex from the box, blow your nose. Nice to have a hanky to squeeze in bed, consoling, a bit like a cuddly toy.

The flannel is soon saturated. The noise starts again.

The Wrong Position: 3.

Still on your back but legs crossed now and hands tucked under your head, like someone lying contentedly under an oak tree at the end of a long picnic in the 1920s. Like Sebastian Flyte in *Brideshead*.

One shin pushes down on the other. It's not going to work.

Which one do you prefer, Anthony Andrews or Jeremy Irons? The young Jeremy! Surely he's the one. That first summer at Brideshead, before it all gets sad and drunk and Catholic. To make one short novel last for twelve episodes! They don't make 'em like that any more. You're thinking in clichés but no one needs to know. You can live every moment of it to the full. The romantic friendship of two young men, so wrapped up in each other that they don't need anyone else. All any of us needs is one friend. One true friend.

Now the music is singing in your head. By Geoffrey Burgon. The tents and khaki uniforms of World War II. Jeremy looking drained of emotion. Until he sees the house. '*I had been there before; I knew all about it.*' Just concentrate on the first two episodes, the Oxford one with the plovers' eggs, and the Venice one. Think about Venice. You could go to sleep thinking about Venice.

Venice.

The sound of the canal water lapping under the
gondola drowns out the sound of the dripping tap.
Not that you've ever been in a gondola. £100 an
hour. A vaporetto, yes.

Can you trace the walk from the hotel to the
Fondamente Nuove where you get the boat to Torcello
and Burano? Not a palazzo, the hotel you stayed in. A drain-
smelling room in which you vomited up the squid-ink spaghetti.
Forget about that. Think of the bridges. Up, along, down. Up, along,
down. Along that touristy alley, follow the signs to the Ospedale, left, right, left,
right, along the wall until you see the lagoon.

You want to be in Venice now. Arrive at the station in the dead of night and walk
into that foggy magical world. Too expensive, though. Running out of money, none left
for holidays in places which have the euro.

Maybe Cornwall, then?

Much cheaper. But not as cheap as all that, and you're probably too late now to book a cottage. Or even a caravan. Or even a space on the campsite.

Rainy days in Cornwall: you've had a few of those. The empty beach with the red flag flying – bathing prohibited. How on earth do you spend a long rainy day in Cornwall? You visit the local stately home, along with a thousand other families in cagoules. You try to be interested in the inlaid desk in the roped-off study, still as it was in 1907, with a cigar propped up in an ashtray. You queue in the converted stable block for a National Trust ham roll.

No. You'll have to go somewhere warm. France? It does have the euro, but surely not as expensive as Venice, no gondolas to be tempted by, and you'll try really hard to be frugal. French motorways are so fast, so empty. You'll zoom past the slate roofs of Burgundy to the red roofs of the south. '*L'autoroute du sud.*' The hardest French phrase to pronounce.

Your husband doesn't get summer holidays like schoolchildren do. He ploughs on through July and August. How can adult life have turned out like that? Supposed to get six weeks, though he never takes them all. But where would you be without his job?

So how will it be when he's made redundant?

Will he hear by email or will he be called up to an office with an 'executive washroom' like the horrible boss has in *The Apartment*? 'I'm afraid we've got to let you go.'

He'll come straight home and you'll have a really nice afternoon. A walk with the dog. Together at last on a weekday. Years since you had a walk together on a Thursday afternoon.

But the bottom would fall out of your life. It would be the end. At least now you crawl towards the 24th, 25th and 26th of each month when money trickles into the account. Not huge amounts, like 'Atlantic breakers rolling in to the Cornish coast', as you've heard bankers' salaries described; but enough to keep you in Andrex, Red Leicester, Cumberland pork chipolatas, Jasmine Hom Mali rice (recommended by Delia for any of the Thai recipes), oak-smoked wafer-thin ham, large free-range eggs, Sky Plus, BT broadband and Royal Canine dried food for the adult neutered dog with a tendency to put on weight.

That money would dry up. 'So much month still left at the end of the money!' There would be years left at the end of the money.

You could happily live on baked potatoes for the rest of your life. But what about the school fees?

Why did you go the private-school route?

A sucker for the uniforms? Perhaps. One of many reasons. Too late to change now. But the fees keep going up and up. And the money you earn goes down and down. There's no one to appeal to about the unfairness of this. The world needs a kind headmaster. 'But Sir! It's unfair!' How much longer can it go on for?

Remember: school fees don't go on for ever. But while you're paying them they seem to. Fifteen years done, nine more to go. The afterthought child. But you wouldn't be without him.

Other people seem to be able to pay theirs. Other people always seem richer. Are they just pretending? Some of them have a whole spare house for holidays. And go skiing every February half-term. Not that you'd want to. Legs dangling off the chair-lift.

2.13 am. Try a bath.

Some people say it works. Back to the bathroom, light a romantic candle for one, make sure the water's running hot before you put the plug in. If you don't do that the cold bottom of the bath never recovers. Don't men get that? They're too busy, minds on higher things. Or lower things.

You get in. Water therapy. Hair wash as well as body wash? Why not? The cold feeling of the blob of shampoo *'pour les cheveux déséchés et très sensibilisés'*. Thank God it's in French, not as depressing as reading a description of one's hair in one's own language. Rub it in, leave it on to do its work, sink back down to rinse.

Your hair's falling out. It's all twirled up round your fingers. Get it off. It's stuck to the soap. You're going bald. For a man that's OK, but for a woman? Keep it secret, get out of the bath now, pull the plug, remove the evidence from the plug-hole. No one must know.

2:36 am. Go and say hello to the dog.

She doesn't have insomnia, so you'll be waking her up. But she'll be thrilled. A fuss made of her in the middle of the night! Oh, the love she gives, the love she laps up. She gazes deeply into your eyes and you gaze deeply into hers. You never do that with a human any more: really gaze. Did you ever do it, even over the candlelit dinner à deux?

But she thinks it's the morning and wants to go out. You unlock the door to the garden and she darts out to do some guarding, using her most scary bark. Waking up the whole street. 'In! Now! It's the middle of the night!' As you shut the door on her she looks at you with the tragic, uncomprehending expression of a parting from the beloved for ever. It's heartbreaking. Because one day it will be for the last time.

The Wrong Position: 4.

Back in bed, with a towel over the pillow for the nearly-dry hair. So comforting, the towel. Your mother used to put one on your pillow when you had flu. Try facing the beloved. He's facing the other way so there's no breath to worry about. Good to give your other side a go. That's the side your heart is on, isn't it? No chance of being able to sleep in this position, but at least it's a change. Push your leg out and feel the rift between the mattresses. In the far distance, feel his leg. Then turn away again.

A third of the world is asleep at any given moment. That's over two billion people. How do they do it?

Should you take a sleeping pill?

You would if you had one. Time to go to the doctor and discuss the symptoms? Maybe you should book an appointment tomorrow. She'll prescribe you something ending in '-diene' or '-nin' and you'll take it and fall into a stupor. The kind of deep, pill-induced sleep that makes you miss hurricanes. Then you'll take it the next night and the next and you'll become addicted like French people do to their sleeping pills. Surely, surely better to try to conquer this naturally? While you're still not taking pills you can pretend there's nothing seriously wrong.

You're in the company of Balzac, a famous non-sleeper in the days before pills. He was so prolific during his sleepless nights that your parents have his complete works which spell out his name, one letter on each spine: HONORE DE BALZAC. Two of the volumes don't have anything on the spine because they are the spaces between the words.

It was those two left-out books that you used to feel sorry for.

Dog loss.

That time when she went out of the door, crossed the main road and was seen being escorted away by a stranger. You got her back. Was he trying to steal her or was she just following him because he had food?

The time when she fell into the pool and scrabbled at the sides to get out, her pathetic little doggy paws, her panic. All pools should have those duck-ramps they have in ponds.

The time when she just vanished. You looked round, in the park, and she wasn't there. Wasn't anywhere. Eventually you found her: she'd settled into a picnic with a group of students who were feeding her M&S miniature pork pies.

The vet. The last time you went, the person whose dog's appointment was just before yours came out from behind the white door sobbing quietly. That'll be you one day. Putting dogs down is so quick, people say. It's all over in a few seconds. The limp body. The empty house. You've got it coming to you.

The broken things.

Broken loo seat, dripping tap, broken lamp, leaky mark on ceiling, downstairs television only works for DVDs, curtain ring missing so when you close one side you open the other, burnt lampshade, right-front gas ring weak, mouse droppings in cupboard under front steps, wobbly kitchen chair, fridge so cold that anything at the back freezes, freezer stuck on -30 so guzzling energy, ripped sofa cover, front door key hard to turn if you don't know the knack, burglar-alarm keypad only works if you jab it, piano pedal squeaks, washing machine smells, cistern problem makes house shake when you flush downstairs loo. It's harder to think of what isn't broken than what is.

But somehow you get used to broken things. You learn to live with them. They become familiar, like old friends.

How do you begin to tackle all this brokenness?

When did you last have sex?

A fortnight ago? 'Once a week is too often, once a month is not enough.' So said a notable Roman Catholic about Confession; and so say you about that. But once a week would be great, if only you got around to it. So much easier just to read your book. Or drift off to sleep in the second half of *Question Time*.

Remember that article saying married couples should put sex in their diaries, along with parents' evenings, dentists' appointments, etc. But that would be so embarrassing. Doesn't anyone realize that even married couples are embarrassed by that kind of thing?

Anyway, it doesn't make you sleep well afterwards. Post-coital insomnia is a rarely discussed phenomenon. He sleeps. You lie awake, feeling wonderful, reliving the highlights, inspired, creative, unpeeled after weeks in the onion skin. There's a difference between being spent and being able to sleep.

So how about waking him up now for a little...

Do people really do that? Wake each other up in the middle of the night? 'Ehem, ehem. Hello, there! Let's, er, you know…' He'd be appalled. And in order to be kind, he'd have to pretend to like it, which would be even worse.

A pity, though. A waste of these empty hours. How often do other married couples…? No one knows. It's the great secret, along with other people's salaries.

'That always works for me.'

That's what your friend said. It's what people always say. But have you noticed? The bath didn't work, did it? Nor did visiting the dog. You're still wide awake.

Other advice you've been given: 'Count backwards in threes. That always works for me.' You tried that yesterday. 500, 497, 494, 491, 488, quite hard, actually, a bit too gymnastic for your ageing brain. Did it work? No. You got as far as 425 and then pretended they were dates in the Dark Ages, and that set you off thinking about the Goths and the Visigoths.

'Try to love your insomnia,' someone else said to you. 'Get up for a while, enjoy the dawn chorus, celebrate the fact that you're awake. Then go back to bed. That always works for me.' You tried that too, earlier in the week. You listened as hard as you could but you couldn't hear any dawn chorus, and that set you off worrying about the declining bird population.

Is advice about how to get to sleep always (a) slightly annoying and (b) destined not to work? The people who give it mean well, but when you hear their advice in your head it sounds smug, as if they're a bit too pleased with their own success and lateral thinking.

And when things that work for other people don't work for you, you start to panic.

Things you've nearly run out of.

Ketchup: the upside-down bottle is mostly transparent now. Just a red smudge at the bottom. Makes a nasty noise when you squirt. Horrible, those bottles which are meant to spend their lives upside down. Not natural, not pretty. Horrible when things are nearly finished. The loo roll when you take those final sheets and get down to the brown cardboard. The cling film when you don't have quite enough to cover the bowl of left-overs. The till receipt when it has pink lines on it to warn that the roll is nearly at an end. All good things come to an end. Life comes to an end.

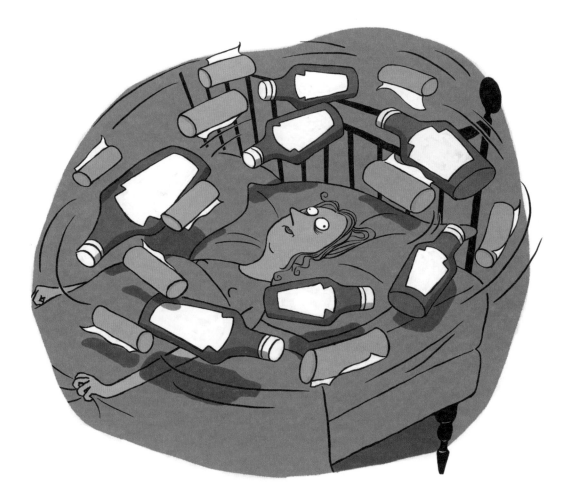

But when?

In bed, aged 94. Please can it be in bed, aged 94? Not in a hospital, aged 53. What is that dull ache at the side of your bosom? The dullest of dull aches. Breast cancer, probably. Go for another mammogram. They make you write a self-addressed envelope for them to send the result back to you in. It's as if you're self-addressing your own death warrant.

Which of the 200 kinds of cancer on the menu are you in fact going to die of? Will it be the ache under the armpit, or the unexplained headache and dizziness, or the persistent chesty cough, or the large mole on the thigh, or the mild tummy ache which turns out to be the 'stealthy killer'? By the time you feel that tummy ache it will be too late. There's a charity called Ovacome for that one, but not many people do overcome it.

Who'll change the lightbulbs when you're dead? Who'll dead-head the roses? Who'll know where the pencil sharpener is?

You can feel your teeth decaying right now.

If you push your bottom teeth against your top teeth, they move. Quite a pleasant sensation, in a way, producing a very soft salival sound. But what it means is that your gums are receding. The dentist did warn you. That's why you so rarely go to the dentist: he warns you of things you don't want to know.

'But I do brush them, every morning and night,' you pleaded the last time you went (must be getting on for a year ago). But not as they should be brushed, said the soft-fingered dentist. He offered to coat your teeth with yellow plaque-displayer. You politely declined. Who wants to be shown their shame? Opening wide for the dentist is as scary as opening wide for God.

3.01 am. The Wrong Position: 5.

Onto your right side again, facing away from the beloved, but this time with the hands up over your head like a horizontal ballerina. Right ear weighing down on right arm. Discard towel: too warm. Pillow newly turned, cold again, bliss. Neck pillow wedged under the neck: an indispensible item as long as it's old and therefore floppy. Pins and needles starting in right arm. No chance of going to sleep like this. Should you get up and go downstairs and do a useful job? Slay a mental block?

Would now be a good time to move the furniture?

The reason you can't sleep is that the sofa in the sitting-room is in the wrong place. It doesn't work in front of the radiator. There's no room for a table with a lamp on it so no one ever sits on that sofa because it's perpetually dark. You could sort that out right now, and then you'd be able to sleep.

Think it through first. You'll go downstairs and switch a light on, grab the sofa by both hands and try to yank it over the loose rug. There'll be a high-pitched squeal of casters. Then there'll be another high-pitched squeal: that will be you stubbing – or perhaps breaking – your toe.

You'll slowly turn the sofa round, by 90 degrees. How much better that will look! Why haven't you got round to doing that in the daylight hours? Clarity comes in the night time.

You never wrote that thank-you letter.

Oh, God. Every day you put off writing it, it gets harder and harder to face. It would now have to begin with a monumental apology, going on for three lines. *'Dear Paul and Sarah, I'm sorry it's taken me so long to put pen to paper, there's no excuse, just the usual thing of being busy with all the chores that clutter up our lives…'* Who'd want to read that stuff? But nor can you begin with *'Dear Paul and Sarah, What a lovely evening we had with you three and a half weeks ago.'* If it was such a lovely evening, why haven't you thanked them? The truth is it was a pretty awful evening. Slabs of steamed white plaice and mashed potatoes… *'Dear Paul and Sarah, Please forgive me for taking so long to thank you for that super evening. You gave us a delicious supper.'* Don't mention how long ago it was. Don't mention the actual food. It's never too late to say thank you. Do it tomorrow.

What's the date tomorrow?

Oh, Christ. It's a week after your godson's birthday. You forgot it again. And his mother never forgets your son's birthday. Her present always arrives two days early. The kindness, the efficiency, how does she do it? Twenty-pound note must go into a card tomorrow and you'll have to use the dreaded word 'belated'. 'A belated happy birthday'. Is that word ever used except in late birthday cards from guilty godparents?

The innocent sleep. It's the bad people like you, with guilty consciences, who lie awake.

What about the goddaughter you've completely lost touch with? Too late to remedy that one. The parents (who used to be your friends) have seen your true colours now. You'll have to face it on the Day of Judgment. 'But they moved away when she was two,' you'll plead. 'Hundreds of miles away.' No excuse. The man (angel?) at the gates will shake his (her?) head. 'You could have posted presents. What stopped you?'

But in order to post a present you have to choose one and wrap it up in wrapping paper and then brown paper (who has brown paper? No one), write the person's address on the front (complete with postcode) and your address on the back and carry it round to the post office and queue up and get it weighed. Twice a year, just for one godchild.

Remember when your babies used to cry in the night?

Your heart literally sank. The pathetic little distress call at 3am: you could actually feel your heart going downwards towards your groin. Interrupted sleep. Stumble out of bed, reach into the cot, take him out, hug his warm body, smell his delicious head mingled with the familiar, bearable-only-to-you smell of his excrement, change the nappy, bring him into your bed – dangerous say some but he never did die of cot death, did he? Feed him with 'nature's packed lunch' (nature's midnight feast) and he went off to sleep; you took him back to his cot and then you went back to sleep.

Now you're never woken in the night by a crying child. How you longed for this time to come! A whole uninterrupted night. Be careful what you wish for. You've got this precious gift but you abuse it. An unforced error, as they say in the Wimbledon commentary.

Wait for the next car to go past.

Here it comes. Getting closer. Louder, louder. Now slowing down for the speed bump. Wait for it…Flump! That's the exhaust pipe being shaken on impact. Or is it the sump? That oil-reservoir thing at the bottom of a car which scrapes against sudden impediments.

You campaigned for those speed bumps. Again, you got what you wished for. The road might be safer for children to cross, but this nocturnal listening out for cars to slow down definitely makes sleep more elusive. Where are these cars going at this time of night? Surely up to no good. Here comes another.

The wrong house?

If you moved to the country you wouldn't be lying awake waiting for the next car. You'd be drifting off to sleep to the sound of a hooting owl. You'd have a boot room. That row of Wellingtons in descending sizes that people always have in the country, the smell of wet coats, a riding hat, a dedicated sink for washing the mud off.

You'd have room for a ping-pong table and a grand piano. A trampoline in the far corner of one of the lawns. Log fire in a huge grate, logs from one of your own trees. Chest freezer full of pheasants. You'd wake up on Saturday mornings in summer and run out into the garden to pick plums for breakfast. Quick swim in the lake.

Why do you live this urban life? And where's that slight draught coming from? Did you remember to double-lock the front door? You must have left something open. That means the weird man can get in. The long-haired one who lives five doors away. There's always one, isn't there? You've seen him staring at you with lidless eyes. He's coming to get you this very night. Carrying an axe. Or a club.

So, put the house on the market tomorrow? Swap it for Woodhill Farm, Dorset, and just keep a small city pad? But even country houses get cordoned off by the police after brutal murders. And you'd spend every Sunday evening in a traffic jam on the A303.

The traffic jam last Saturday.

You allowed two and a half hours to get to your son's concert. Two and a half hours to go 60 miles. The open road at 80mph, listening to The Best of Nanci Griffith CD, married, parental, the world opening up in front of you as it did when you fell in love. Then the inexplicable slowing down to walking pace. Life's possibilities suddenly becoming life's impossibilities. Ten miles to the next exit. Slight pressure on the bladder. On a motorway, you're trapped.

'They ought to open up the hard shoulder at times like this.' How many times has he said that? But he's right. A shameful waste of that empty lane. Just as wasted as this empty hour of the night.

The cars going the other way are detestably smug. How dare they drive at 80mph when you're stuck? And their drivers are omniscient. They know what you're in for. How long? How long? How long?

It's one thing to go slowly: frustrating but bearable. It's another to go slowly and be late for the precious thing you're taking three hours to get to.

And you were late. You missed it. It's gone.

You let out a deep gutteral sigh and get out of bed.

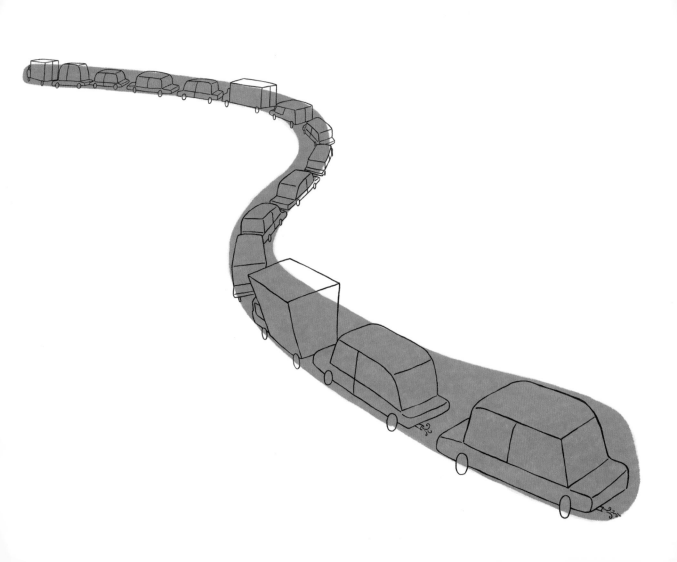

3.42am. Down to the kitchen.

Dishwasher finished its cycle hours ago. Its front panel still warm, recovering from its 156-minute ordeal. Open the fridge out of curiosity. The sight of the hard, grey chunks of lamb cut off the bone last Sunday make you feel sick. Close the fridge so hard that the magnets slide down a millimetre. Those magnets have been there far too long.

Survey the fruit bowl. In *Sleepless in Seattle* Meg Ryan peeled a super-sized American Granny Smith apple all in one as she relived Tom Hanks saying 'It was like… magic.' The young Tom Hanks, so gorgeous. Pulling the wall map down to show Jonah how far Seattle is from Baltimore.

You can't face an apple. The thought of its bitter juice gives you an acute gastric-juice stomach ache. You've heard it helps to drink a cup of warm milk or milky decaffeinated tea to get you to sleep. No thanks. It would put too much pressure on the bladder. And too much pressure on you to get to sleep in the small window of opportunity before the soporific effect is trumped by the diuretic effect.

Small glass of water. You sit at the table, head on hands, like a child asleep during a physics lesson. What are you doing here, in this silent downstairs place? You reach inside your bag for your phone. Emails: 2. That sight always makes the heart beat faster. Will it be something flattering which nudges forward the plot of the gripping novel which is your life?

It's not. Just middle-of-the-night off-peak emails from businesses. 'Important information about your broadband usage.' 'iTunes Store.' They use your first name to make you feel they care.

You can hear a scuffling sound. It's the mouse, on his night-time rounds. The mouse man has been to bait the house with poisoned peanut butter and you're terrified of the dog getting at it by mistake. The mouse seems to be thriving on it.

You look at the clock on the wall: 3.55. Grope your way upstairs.

3.56 am. The wrong bed.

Try the spare bed in the boys' room. Bring the radio with you for company. Enchanting to be in the same room as the sleeping boys. Their sweet breathing on the upper bunk and the lower bunk. The radio won't wake them. Here you can break wind uninhibitedly and flap the smell upwards towards your nose. Why does one's own flatulence smell so good? It makes no sense.

Try Radio 5 Live. 'Up All Night' is the name of the programme. The presenters get paid for it, though. They clock off at five, then home to black-out blinds in the bedroom. It's a phone-in. Who phones in at this time of the night? Truck-drivers, mostly. Reassuring, gruff voices holding forth on the football transfer window. They should soothe you. Think of a truck-drivers' caff on the A1. Baked-bean breakfasts. Paunches. Think of Eddie Stobart. He died much too young.

It's freezing in this spare bed. The bottom end is still as unexplored as Greenland. Too cold to go there. Who slept in this bed last? A sleepover last Friday and you didn't change the sheets. The pillow smells mildly of the boy's unwashed hair. This is a synthetic duvet, stuffed with kapok. Cheaper than Hungarian goose down. It was mean of you to buy a cheap one for this bed.

And how are your children going to earn their millions?

Or their thousands. Or even their hundreds. Or even get a part-time job in a pub? How on earth do you get your toe in the door of a career these days? Youth unemployment over a million. Hard even to get work experience. Perhaps they'll live at home for the rest of their lives, on £20 a week each. You could all huddle together for warmth and live on omelettes and at least you wouldn't be paying school fees any more.

'You mustn't live through your children,' a wise friend told you, and she's right. But you can't help it. Their successes are yours, and so are their failures. What if they get sacked, or divorced? How will you bear it? What if they expect you to be an unpaid full-time nanny to their children because they're so busy trying to earn their thousands or their hundreds? You see those exploited, exhausted-looking grannies pushing pushchairs in the park for hours on end. Will that be you one day?

Please God can your children be happy and fulfilled? 'You're only as happy as your saddest child.' Yes.

'You know what's happened, don't you?'

Now you're thinking of *Brief Encounter*. The film you think of more than any other. It's the quintessence of sadness.

Celia Johnson does know what's happened. Trevor Howard has fallen in love with her. And she has fallen in love too, though they're both officially happily married. They meet exactly nine times. And then they part for ever. The squeeze of the shoulder in the station tea-room. A parting like death. Worse than death, because they have to live with the loss for the rest of their lives.

Would it be better if they had never met? Or worse?

'I want to die.'

'If you died, you'd forget me. I want to be remembered.'

The Rachmaninov music is now blaring in your head, Eileen Joyce at the piano.

Try to think of something happy.

OK, here goes. An English meadow in May. Lying on the grass among the dandelions and buttercups. Punnet of pick-your-own strawberries to share. The picnic rug, laid out across the grass, made slightly mountainous by tussocks. Look down at the pretty village below, with its church tower. England at its most perfect. Blue and white sky, scudding clouds.

You're doing it. You're thinking of something happy! You can even start counting the sheep. Pretend they're jumping over the stile in the corner. (Do sheep really jump over stiles? Surely the whole point is that they can't.)

Just have them jumping over that low jump for ponies. One, two, three, four. Come on, little lamb. You can do it. That's it! Over you go!

This isn't working.

Well try to think of something sad, then.

Easy to tap into your Saddest Thought Ever, which unites two of your chief anxieties. It's dogs in the Holocaust. The family pet of those families who were woken in the middle of the night. What happened to the dogs? Were they just left in the flat to wake up without their master? Were they shot on the spot? What would you do to your own dog? The last hug. Were they just let out, to become feral and hunt in great packs of abandoned loved ones, across Vienna and Berlin?

You should investigate and write a book about it. It would definitely be eligible for the prize for Saddest Book Ever Written.

Unthink the thought of it happening to your own dog.

But you can't unthink it.

Instead, you smother the thought by thinking of something worse and more up-to-date. Your child being knocked off a bike, killed in an instant by White Van Man. The policeman arriving at your front door.

One mistake and you're dead. How many times have you reminded them to be careful? Wear a helmet. Treat every single passing car as a potential murderer. 'Yeah, yeah.' But it's true. It happens every day. It could be your child.

You'd have to choose the hymns for the funeral. Not 'Abide with me'. For those in peril on the road.

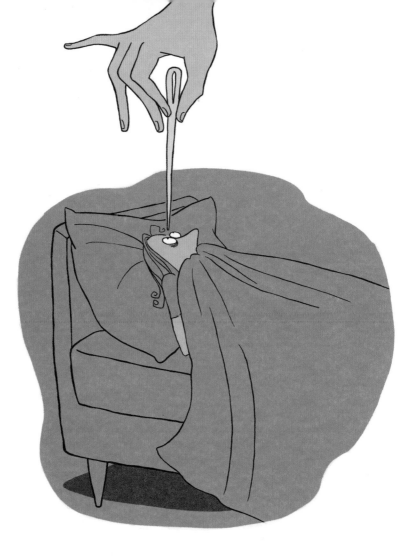

Deeper into pain.

The only way to unthink such a thought is to counter-attack it by thinking of something toxically terrible of a different kind. OK, think of the most distressing pain ever. Easy: a needle right through the middle of your eye. You once thought of that, ten years ago, and it has haunted your thoughts ever since. An embroidery needle, right through the retina.

So exquisitely horrible that you rub your eyes vigorously and gasp. Time to go back to your own bed. You steal out of the boys' room, listening to their breathing for reassurance, and go back to where you belong.

The Wrong Position: 6. Home again.

Enough! Banish all that horror. The bliss of being back in your own warm inhabited bed, such a relief it makes you want to cry. Face towards him, curled up into a ball, foetal position, like the subject of a 20-week-scan photo. Feet gradually warming up – tempting to warm them faster by shoving them under his sleeping frame, but that would be a nasty cold shock for him.

Imagine you're still in your mother's womb, curled up like this, your tiny heart beating vigorously, your mother's slower heartbeat booming nearby. You managed to sleep in those days. Except when you were awake and kicking.

Thinking of kicking makes you need to kick out. A bit of the old Restless-Leg Syndrome which dogged your pregnancies. You turn round on your separate mattress and kick manically for ten seconds. You feel such a surge of energy that you want to get out of bed and run to the sea. What time does the gym open? Not for three hours. You look at the digital clock on the radio: 4.03am. The *Today* programme team will have arrived at Broadcasting House.

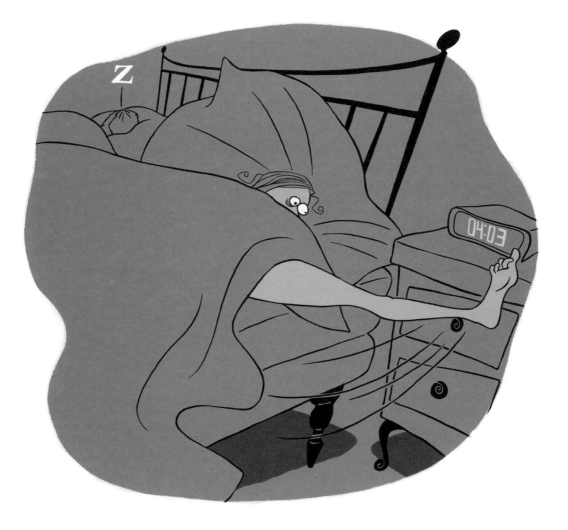

Why haven't you been to the gym recently?

Blame the dog. It's pointless expending a calorie of physical energy when you're not making the dog expend her energy, too. You'd come home from the gym exhausted and she'd be hyper-active and you'd have to start all over again.

But what's happening to your core muscles? They must be rotting from lack of use.

OK, do some core-muscle work now. Put this time to good use. Squeeze the pelvic floor. Squeeze. And again. Harder. Clench the buttocks. Such a pleasing and intrinsically funny word, 'buttock'. Nick Clarke used it in his beautiful voice in that programme he made about getting cancer. 'My left buttock.' 'I knew the game was up.' And it was.

SQUEEZE!

04:18

At least you don't have to do school games any more.

That's the one great consolation of adulthood. Clenching your buttocks in bed, though moderately demanding, is better than standing on a pitch holding a stick and trying to chase a ball. In the rain. Those endless afternoons you spent on pitches! Looking at your watch which said ten-past two. The yelling games teacher with her whistle.

And remember those team games, where the captains picked their teams. You were always last to be picked. In fact, everyone you've ever heard on *Desert Island Discs* talking about that experience remembers being the last to be picked. That must mean that only people who were last to be picked are interesting enough to be interviewed in later life. Good.

It's a games day for your son tomorrow. Have you got the games bag ready? The mouthguard in its plastic box? Disgusting thing, covered in mud and saliva, and you're forced to buy one. The mouthguard company must be making millions.

4.39am. Time to look out of the window.

You leap out of bed, pull up the blind and open the window as wide as you can. Check that the weird axe-wielder isn't loafing around. If he saw you in your nightie you'd be dead meat. No, no one there. The cool air on your cheeks! In thy dark streets shineth the everlasting streetlight. An urban fox darts past across the road. Rubbish sacks piled up on the pavement: the lorry will arrive soon to take away your unshredded paperwork. You should get a shredder. The pasta-maker for paper. Any glimpse of dawn in the east? Not yet.

You long for dawn but you also dread it. Because then you'll have to get up and live through a day. How will you manage that? Sleep-deprivation is one of the most-feared forms of torture. You'll feel jet-lagged, ill, confused, sick, helpless, you won't be able to make clear decisions, you'll betray your friends to the Stasi. You'll have to keep yourself awake with coffee until you shake.

Time to reach for the dressing gown.

And the slippers to go with it. Downstairs to the sofa, switch the lamp on, tuck a rug under your feet and reach for the nearest book, which happens to be *The Hobbit*. Fiddle with rug's woolly tassels as you read, plait them together. Lovely, Tolkien's Anglo-Saxon words, the world of the Shire, the sweetness of the dwarves. Oin and Gloin. But your eyes hurt. Your head aches. You nod. Was that a nod of agreement or was it an accidental nod of sleep?

Back to bed, quick. The right Position:1.

You might be able to recapture that nod. Fling dressing-gown on to chair, covering yesterday's cast-off clothes, kick off slippers, back into bed, get straight into most-likely-to-induce-sleep position, on your side. Think of the calm Shire and Oin and Gloin. Think of the furry feet of the hobbits and the kettle boiling in the hobbit hole.

Your son is meant to be writing a book review of it.

Due next Monday. Needless to say nearly everyone else in the class has already written their *Hobbit* review. 'Give a brief description of the plot and main characters.' Why have you never had a swotty child? Someone who comes home and says, 'Please can I do my homework now?' How will he get into his next school? The competition! Young hopefuls from all over the city, every one a rival. Two hundred trying for 30 places. It's got to come from him. He's got to want to do well. The verbal reasoning test! Even worse, the non-verbal reasoning test. 'What's the next picture in the series?' He has no idea, and nor do you. Something to do with rotating the picture by 45 degrees... Are these things truly a test of one's intelligence? He knows the stories of the kings and queens of England. He really minds about Edward VI dying at fifteen. Isn't that enough?

5.05am. The front gate opens.

It's the newspaper being delivered. Today's crop of births, marriages and deaths. You always look at the deaths first these days, just to make sure there's no one you know. And usually they're all total strangers. You've hardly even heard of the people who have obituaries. Famous but not famous to you. Great lives – and you've missed them. You look at the ages, sighing with relief at 'aged 86 years', and shuddering at 'suddenly' and 'aged 49'. Always fewer births than deaths, though the population's growing and the roads are going to be 50 per cent more congested in 20 years' time. You'll have to allow four hours to get to the concert then.

Your friend who died aged 22. 'Suddenly aged 22.' You think of her every single day. If she were still alive, maybe you wouldn't think of her nearly as much. You might even have lost touch with her. But, dead, she's perpetually close to your heart. You can treasure her, nurse the memory of her, be inspired daily by her. She introduced you to many of your favourite pieces of music.

I once had a whim and I had to obey it…

'To buy a French horn in a second-hand shop. I polished it up and I started to play it...' No, not that Flanders and Swann one, please. If you've ever heard a piece of orchestral music put to words you can never hear it again without singing those words. *This is the second theme, the second theme of the 'Unfinished'. It must be jelly, it must be jelly, 'cos raspberry jam never tasted like that.* The sublime music of Mozart, Schubert and Beethoven, all reduced to ditties.

Stop this cacophony. Think of a Beatles song. *I am the eggman, I am the eggman, I am the Walrus, goo-goo-ga-joob.* That'll do. Bad idea to read the lyrics of that one. It sounds more like 'Coo-coo-cha-choo' but the CD booklet says it's definitely 'goo-goo-ga-joob'. Some things are best not written down.

Now that song is lodged in your brain, claiming squatter's rights. You can't evict it. You'll just have to join it. 'The Beatles are dying in the wrong order.' Now, there's a thought to ponder.

What's that smell?

Of course. It's the bread. You set the bread-maker yesterday evening, with a seven-hour time delay. A Christmas present you've been feeling guilty about not using enough. And this is exactly why you don't use it. If you use it in the daytime the sound is deafening, a great grinding, churning sound making it impossible to coexist with it in the kitchen. And if you use it at night, the smell at dawn is overpowering. Heat rises, smell rises, and up they both come, straight into the bedroom. Heavy, yeasty, warm, unbearable. Supposed to sell a house, the smell of fresh bread or coffee. Well, it might sell a house but it won't let you sleep in it.

You get up and close the bedroom door firmly. You look at the bolt on the door, put there purely to enable marital relations to exist in a family setting. It was quite embarrassing even asking the handyman to put the bolt on.

5:29am. The Wrong Position: 7.

On your haunches, bent right over, face touching the mattress, as if you're responding to
a muezzin calling the faithful to prayer in Damascus. Of course this isn't going to work,
but it's certainly refreshing. And it's stretching a few neglected muscles. It feels more like
a gesture of despair than of prayer. But try praying, anyway. 'Dear God, please find me
the right position, one that works, and please defend me from all the perils
and dangers of this night. Please. I'm desperate.'

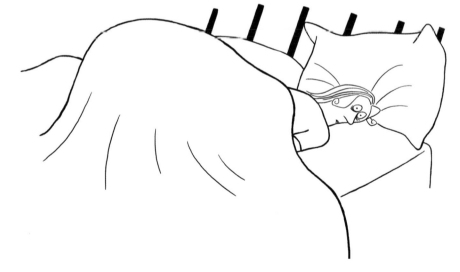

If at first you don't succeed,

Try, try again. You've always been taught, and you teach your children, that if you really try hard at something you can do it. But that's not true with sleep. The very act of trying hard to do it makes it impossible.

A bit like trying to find someone to marry. If you try too hard you'll never meet him. But if you just amble nonchalantly through life, accepting the occasional dinner invitation but not caring too much, it might happen. Desperation is a turn-off, and that must be what sleep thinks of you: she's desperate, so no thanks. You must play harder-to-get. You're certainly being hard-to-get in this Islamic prayer position.

Who else is awake?

So many people. Everyone in California (not bedtime yet) and in Asia (this afternoon already). Nurses in hospitals, people giving birth, people groaning and calling for water. The homeless, waking with cold in the subway, their slab of cardboard not thick enough. The Tesco workers around the corner: 'Now open 24 hours!' Migrant workers packing chicken breasts in Suffolk warehouses. When they finish their shift they have to wait ages for a minibus to take them away. Horizontal non-sleepers like you all over the country, longing for but dreading dawn, like the soldiers on the eve of Agincourt. If someone tore the roofs off all the houses in this terrace, would it reveal a long row of parallel insomniac bodies, lined up as if in a barracks?

The Wrong Position: 8.

Lie on your back in the 'star' position, legs stretched out at a 70-degree angle and arms likewise above your head. Take me, day – I'm yours! You stare up at the ceiling. You feel flattened out, like a dissected frog. A scientist could lean over you and lift out your liver and kidneys, and your intestines and pancreas.

Your St Pancreas Station. The first Eurostar of the day will be leaving for Paris now. Businessmen going for a meeting at a bank in the 16th arrondissement. The dull 16th. You'd much rather live in the 6th. Near the Seine. 'People who throw themselves into the river in Paris are insane.' One from your son's pun collection. Your mind is wandering. You're getting sleepy.

5·40am. Men's voices outside.

The sound of the lids being taken off your dustbins and the bags being lifted out one by one. Such an uplifting early-morning sound that you jump out of bed again and peep through the curtains at the men. Yes, they're up and about, in gloves. You're tempted to open the window and jump out into their burly arms, overjoyed to be in the company of awake people. And soon round the corner comes the great whining lorry, and your discarded paper and plastic is borne away, don't think where and don't start getting sentimental, this is not the time for it. Recycling sacks separated from black ones, thrown into different sides. Good riddance to the mayonnaise jar, the paper-towel cylinders, the Lands' End catalogue, the packaging for the perfectly ripe avocados. As the great vehicle grinds and moans and then revs up and leaves, you feel purged, cleansed, light-headed.

The bread smell seems to have reached its climax. Perhaps it's got to the cooling stage.

Farming Today.

You switch on the radio. A cattle farm in Norfolk. You can hear the mud. The man who's talking is definitely wearing a Barbour. He sounds nice. So civilised, to have this programme at 5.45. Until all the farmers commit suicide it will go on, you hope. The minutes tick by towards 6 o'clock. The beloved 6 o'clock. At last, it comes. 'Good morning: welcome to the *Today* programme.' Morning has broken! You got there!

6am. The pressure's off.

Too late to sleep now. You'll have to do without it. Listen to the news read by Harriet Cass.

And because you no longer seek sleep, it comes. The delicious, helpless sinking into unconsciousness. Broken momentarily by a car alarm going off in the street. It cuts out after a few seconds and you're sucked back into that beautiful country, the land of dreams. Sweet, sweet stories flow through your sleeping mind. You're far, far away, in perfect comfort, in perfect bliss. You're being healed. Your body and mind are being given what they crave. Deeper, deeper you go down. Your home, your rest.

Beep-beep-beep-beep-beep-beep-beep-beep.

What the fuck's that? The radio alarm. For God's sake, stop it. You grope for the button. Radio comes on. 'It's 7.25 and time for sport with Rob Bonnet.' Last night's results. How can he be so chirpy? How can it be the morning? Just don't disturb me, you want to say, just as when the air hostess brings you a breakfast muffin three hours after supper on the night flight to London from New York. Go away. Leave me alone.

But you must get up. The working day has begun. Astonishingly, as you get out of bed after three and a half hours' less sleep than Margaret Thatcher lived on, you don't feel too bad. You stumble downstairs and make a cup of tea in the favoured mug.

'Morning, darling. Sleep well?'

Ysenda Maxtone Graham made her name as an interviewer for *Harpers & Queen* and *Tatler*. She is the author of *The Real Mrs Miniver*, about the life of her grandmother Jan Struther, which was shortlisted for the Whitbread Biography award; and more recently the acclaimed memoir, *Mr Tibbits's Catholic School*.

Kath Walker is renowned for her brilliantly evocative illustrations. She illustrated Ysenda's weekly column in the *Sunday Express Magazine*, and did the drawings for *Mr Tibbits's Catholic School*. She has worked for numerous clients, including Nivea, Google and Cadburys, and has also illustrated several books, including *Yoga for Cats* and *Pilates for Dogs*.